disc

TABLE OF CONTENTS

WHAT WAS ANKYLOSAURUS?

Ankylosaurus (an-kuh-low-SAWR-uss) was a big, bulky dinosaur. Its name means "stiff **lizard**." *Ankylosaurus* was covered with thick plates. The plates formed a coat of armor. With all that armor, *Ankylosaurus* could not wiggle around much. This dinosaur really *was* stiff!

Ankylosaurus *had strong armor. This protected it from enemies.*

WHAT DID ANKYLOSAURUS LOOK LIKE?

Ankylosaurus was heavy and wide. It weighed about as much as an elephant. It was almost as long as a school bus!

Ankylosaurus *was long and heavy, but it was not very tall.*

Its **skull** bones were very thick. They left only enough room for a tiny brain. So *Ankylosaurus* was not a very smart dinosaur.

Ankylosaurus had four short legs. It had a club on the end of its tail. Other animals did not bother *Ankylosaurus* very often. They did not want to get smacked with the club!

Ankylosaurus had a thick skull (above). *This kept its brain safe from injury. Although bigger dinosaurs tried to eat Ankylosaurus (right), it was good at protecting itself.*

WHAT ABOUT THOSE PLATES?

Ankylosaurus had bony plates on its back and tail. It had plates covering the top of its head. It even had little plates around its eyes!

An Ankylosaurus' plates covered its weakest body parts. The plates not only looked like rocks (above), they were as hard as rocks.

Hard **spines** stood up from the back plates. They stuck out from the head plates. They pointed out sideways from the shoulder plates. Plates and spines were everywhere! What were they for? They protected *Ankylosaurus* from other dinosaurs. Nothing could bite into that armor!

An Ankylosaurus' ***skeleton*** *was made of many different bones.*

13

HOW DID ANKYLOSAURUS SPEND ITS TIME?

Ankylosaurus spent a lot of time eating. It had a big body to feed!

This dinosaur ate plants. Its head hung close to the ground. It could reach plenty of ferns and **shrubs** there. *Ankylosaurus* also had short, wide teeth. They ground up leaves, roots, and sticks.

Ankylosaurus *was a plant eater, so it only fought to defend itself.*

15

HOW DO WE KNOW ABOUT *ANKYLOSAURUS?*

Ankylosaurus lived millions of years ago. So how do we know about it? We know because it left behind some bones and spines. **Scientists** have found them buried in the ground. They have even found *Ankylosaurus* tail clubs!

Barnum Brown (left) was a scientist who studied dinosaurs. He found the first Ankylosaurus bones in Montana and gave the dinosaur its name. He is seen here in Wyoming in 1934.

18

Things that **ancient** animals and plants have left behind are called **fossils**. Fossils tell us where dinosaurs lived. They tell us what kinds of food they ate. Fossils tell us all about *Ankylosaurus*!

Fossils of plants, such as this fern (left), can show what foods dinosaurs may have eaten. Ankylosaurus *might have enjoyed an* Araucaria *cone (above).*

WHERE HAVE ANKYLOSAURUS BONES BEEN FOUND?

Alberta, Canada

Montana

Wyoming

NORTH AMERICA

Atlantic Ocean

Pacific Ocean

EUROPE

ASIA

AFRICA

SOUTH AMERICA

Indian Ocean

AUSTRALIA

Map Key

Where *Ankylosaurus* bones have been found

Where possible *Ankylosaurus* fossils or tracks have been found

Bolivia

Southern Ocean

WHO FINDS THE BONES?

Fossil hunters find dinosaur bones. Some fossil hunters are scientists. Others are people who hunt fossils for fun. They go to areas where dinosaurs once lived. They find bones in rocky places, in mountainsides, and in deserts.

When fossil hunters discover dinosaur bones, they get busy. They use picks to chip rocks away from the fossils. They use small brushes to sweep off any dirt. They take pictures of the fossils. They also write notes about where the fossils were found. They want to remember everything!

Fossil hunters use many tools to dig up fossils. It is very important to use the right tools so the fossils do not get damaged.

GLOSSARY

ancient *(AYN-shunt)* Ancient things are those that existed a very long time ago.

Ankylosaurus *(an-kuh-low-SAWR-uss) Ankylosaurus* was a large dinosaur covered with spiny plates.

fossils *(FOSS-ullz)* Fossils are preserved parts of plants and animals that died long ago.

lizard *(LIZ-urd)* A lizard is a scaly animal that walks on four legs.

scientists *(SY-un-tists)* Scientists are people who study how things work through observations and experiments.

shrubs *(SHRUBZ)* Shrubs are short plants with woody branches and small leaves.

skeleton *(SKEL-uh-tun)* The skeleton is the set of bones in a person or animal's body.

skull *(SKUHL)* The skull is the set of bones in the head.

spines *(SPYNZ)* Spines are sharp, pointed structures.

BOOKS

Birch, Robin. *Bony-skinned Dinosaurs.*
New York: Chelsea House Publishers, 2008.

Galvin, Laura Gates. *Ankylosaurus.*
Norwalk, CT: Soundprints, 2007.

My Terrific Dinosaur Book. New York: DK Publishing, 2008.

Wallace, Karen. *I Am an Ankylosaurus.*
New York: Atheneum Books for Young Readers, 2005.

WEB SITES

Visit our Web site for lots of links about *Ankylosaurus*:
CHILDSWORLD.COM/LINKS

Note to Parents, Teachers, and Librarians: We routinely verify our Web links to make sure they are safe, active sites—so encourage your readers to check them out!

INDEX

ABOUT THE AUTHOR

Susan Gray has written more than ninety books for children. She especially likes to write about animals. Susan lives in Cabot, Arkansas, with her husband, Michael, and many pets.

ABOUT THE ILLUSTRATOR

Robert Squier has been drawing dinosaurs ever since he could hold a crayon. Today, instead of using crayons, he uses pencils, paint, and the computer. Robert lives in New Hampshire with his wife, Jessica, and a house full of dinosaur toys. *Stegosaurus* is his favorite dinosaur.

INTRODUCING DINOSAURS

ANKYLOSAURUS

BY SUSAN H. GRAY · ILLUSTRATED BY ROBERT SQUIER

The Child's World

Published by The Child's World®
1980 Lookout Drive • Mankato, MN 56003-1705
800-599-READ • www.childsworld.com

ACKNOWLEDGMENTS
The Child's World®: Mary Berendes, Publishing Director
The Design Lab: Kathleen Petelinsek, Art Direction and Design;
Victoria Stanley and Anna Petelinsek, Page Production
Editorial Directions: E. Russell Primm, Editor; Lucia Raatma, Copy Editor;
Dina Rubin, Proofreader; Tim Griffin, Indexer

PHOTO CREDITS
©Kamchatka/Dreamstime.com: cover, 2–3; ©Francois Gohier/Photo
Researchers, Inc.: 8, 11, 12–13, 19 (right); ©Bettman/Corbis: 16–17; © Kevin
Schafer/Corbis: 18–19

LIBRARY OF CONGRESS CATALOGING-IN-PUBLICATION DATA
Gray, Susan Heinrichs.
  Ankylosaurus / by Susan H. Gray; illustrated by Robert Squier.
    p. cm.—(Introducing dinosaurs)
  Includes bibliographical references and index.
  ISBN 978-1-60253-235-9 (lib. bound: alk. paper)
  1. Ankylosaurus—Juvenile literature. I. Squier, Robert, ill. II. Title. III. Series.
  QE862.O65G7452 2009
  567.915—dc22   2009001621

Printed in the United States of America
Mankato, Minnesota
May, 2010
PA02063